# Francis Frith's
# Norwich

19.

*Photographic Memories*

# Francis Frith's
# Norwich

Revised edition of original work by

## Martin Andrew

FRITH
BOOK Co

Revised paperback edition published in the United Kingdom in 2000 by
Frith Book Company Ltd

First published in the United Kingdom in 1998
by WBC Ltd

British Library Cataloguing in Publication Data

Francis Frith's Norwich
Martin Andrew
ISBN 1-85937-194-9

Frith Book Company Ltd
Frith's Barn, Teffont,
Salisbury, Wiltshire SP3 5QP
Tel: +44 (0) 1722 716 376
Email: info@frithbook.co.uk
www.frithbook.co.uk


Printed and bound in Great Britain

Front Cover: Rampant Horse Street looking North-West 1891  28163

# Contents

# Francis Frith: *Victorian Pioneer*

**FRANCIS FRITH**, Victorian founder of the world-famous photographic archive, was a complex and multitudinous man. A devout Quaker and a highly successful Victorian businessman, he was both philosophic by nature and pioneering in outlook.

By 1855 Francis Frith had already established a wholesale grocery business in Liverpool, and sold it for the astonishing sum of £200,000, which is the equivalent today of over £15,000,000. Now a multi-millionaire, he was able to indulge his passion for travel. As a child he had pored over travel books written by early explorers, and his fancy and imagination had been stirred by family holidays to the sublime mountain regions of Wales and Scotland. 'What a land of spirit-stirring and enriching scenes and places!' he had written. He was to return to these scenes of grandeur in later years to 'recapture the thousands of vivid and tender memories', but with a different purpose. Now in his thirties, and captivated by the new science of photography, Frith set out on a series of pioneering journeys to the Nile regions that occupied him from 1856 until 1860.

## Intrigue and Adventure

He took with him on his travels a specially-designed wicker carriage that acted as both dark-room and sleeping chamber. These far-flung journeys were packed with intrigue and adventure. In his life story, written when he was sixty-three, Frith tells of being held captive by bandits, and of fighting 'an awful midnight battle to the very point of surrender with a deadly pack of hungry, wild dogs'. Sporting flowing Arab costume, Frith arrived at Akaba by camel seventy years before Lawrence, where he encountered 'desert princes and rival sheikhs, blazing with jewel-hilted swords'.

During these extraordinary adventures he was assiduously exploring the desert regions bordering the Nile and patiently recording the antiquities and peoples with his camera. He was the first photographer to venture beyond the sixth cataract. Africa was still the mysterious 'Dark Continent', and Stanley and Livingstone's historic meeting was a decade into the future. The conditions for picture taking confound belief. He laboured for hours in his wicker dark-room in the sweltering heat of the desert, while the volatile chemicals fizzed dangerously in their trays. Often he was forced to work in remote tombs and caves where conditions were cooler. Back in London he exhibited his photographs and was 'rapturously cheered' by members of the Royal Society. His reputation as a photographer was made overnight. An eminent modern historian has likened their impact on the population of the time to that on our own generation of the first photographs taken on the surface of the moon.

## Venture of a Life-Time

Characteristically, Frith quickly spotted the opportunity to create a new business as a specialist publisher of photographs. He lived in an era of immense and sometimes violent change. For the poor in the early part of Victoria's reign work was a drudge and the hours long, and people had precious little free time to enjoy themselves. Most had no transport other than a cart or gig at their disposal, and had not travelled far beyond the

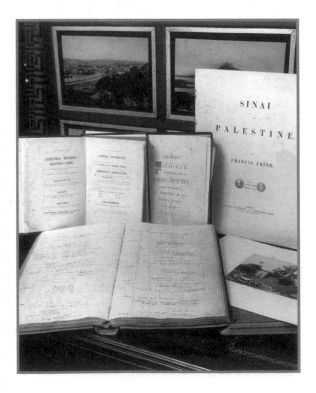

boundaries of their own town or village. However, by the 1870s, the railways had threaded their way across the country, and Bank Holidays and half-day Saturdays had been made obligatory by Act of Parliament. All of a sudden the ordinary working man and his family were able to enjoy days out and see a little more of the world.

With characteristic business acumen, Francis Frith foresaw that these new tourists would enjoy having souvenirs to commemorate their days out. In 1860 he married Mary Ann Rosling and set out with the intention of photographing every city, town and village in Britain. For the next thirty years he travelled the country by train and by pony and trap, producing fine photographs of seaside resorts and beauty spots that were keenly bought by millions of Victorians. These prints were painstakingly pasted into family albums and pored over during the dark nights of winter, rekindling precious memories of summer excursions.

## The Rise of Frith & Co

Frith's studio was soon supplying retail shops all over the country. To meet the demand he gathered about him a small team of photographers, and published the work of independent artist-photographers of the calibre of Roger Fenton and Francis Bedford. In order to gain some understanding of the scale of Frith's business one only has to look at the catalogue issued by Frith & Co in 1886: it runs to some 670 pages, listing not only many thousands of views of the British Isles but also many photographs of most European countries, and China, Japan, the USA and

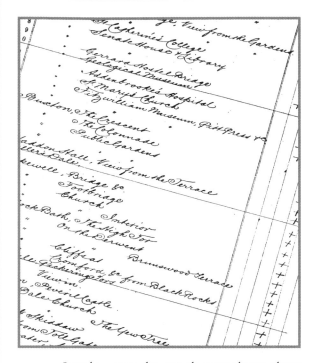

Canada – note the sample page shown above from the hand-written *Frith & Co* ledgers detailing pictures taken. By 1890 Frith had created the greatest specialist photographic publishing company in the world, with over 2,000 outlets – more than the combined number that Boots and W H Smith have today! The picture on the right shows the *Frith & Co* display board at Ingleton in the Yorkshire Dales. Beautifully constructed with mahogany frame and gilt inserts, it could display up to a dozen local scenes.

## Postcard Bonanza

The ever-popular holiday postcard we know today took many years to develop. In 1870 the Post Office issued the first plain cards, with a pre-printed stamp on one face. In 1894 they allowed other publishers' cards to be sent through the mail with an attached adhesive halfpenny stamp. Demand grew rapidly, and in 1895 a new size of postcard was permitted called the court card, but there was little room for illustration. In 1899, a year after Frith's death, a new card measuring 5.5 x 3.5 inches became the standard format, but it was not until 1902 that the divided back came into being, with address and message on one face and a full-size illustration on the other. *Frith & Co* were in the vanguard of postcard development, and Frith's sons Eustace and Cyril continued their father's monumental task, expanding the number of views offered to the public and recording more and more places in Britain, as the coasts and countryside were opened up to mass travel.

Francis Frith died in 1898 at his villa in Cannes, his great project still growing. The archive he created continued in business for another seventy years. By 1970 it contained over a third of a million pictures of 7,000 cities, towns and villages. The massive photographic record Frith has left to us stands as a living monument to a special and very remarkable man.

# Frith's Archive: *A Unique Legacy*

**FRANCIS FRITH'S** legacy to us today is of immense significance and value, for the magnificent archive of evocative photographs he created provides a unique record of change in 7,000 cities, towns and villages throughout Britain over a century and more. Frith and his fellow studio photographers revisited locations many times down the years to update their views, compiling for us an enthralling and colourful pageant of British life and character.

We tend to think of Frith's sepia views of Britain as nostalgic, for most of us use them to conjure up memories of places in our own lives with which we have family associations. It often makes us forget that to Francis Frith they were records of daily life as it was actually being lived in the cities, towns and villages of his day. The Victorian age was one of great and often bewildering change for ordinary people, and though the pictures evoke an impression of slower times, life was as busy and hectic as it is today.

We are fortunate that Frith was a photographer of the people, dedicated to recording the minutiae of everyday life. For it is this sheer wealth of visual data, the painstaking chronicle of changes in dress, transport, street layouts, buildings, housing, engineering and landscape that captivates us so much today. His remarkable images offer us a powerful link with the past and with the lives of our ancestors.

## Today's Technology

Computers have now made it possible for Frith's many thousands of images to be accessed almost instantly. In the Frith archive today, each photograph is carefully 'digitised' then stored on a CD Rom. Frith archivists can locate a single photograph amongst thousands within seconds. Views can be catalogued and sorted under a variety of categories of place and content to the immediate benefit of researchers.

Inexpensive reference prints can be created for them at the touch of a mouse button, and a wide range of books and other printed materials assembled and published for a wider, more general readership - in the next twelve months over a hundred Frith local history titles will be published! The day-to-day workings of the archive are very different from how they were in Francis Frith's time: imagine the herculean task of sorting through eleven tons of glass negatives as Frith had to do to locate a particular

**See Frith at www. frithbook.co.uk**

sequence of pictures! Yet the archive still prides itself on maintaining the same high standards of excellence laid down by Francis Frith, including the painstaking cataloguing and indexing of every view.

It is curious to reflect on how the internet now allows researchers in America and elsewhere greater instant access to the archive than Frith himself ever enjoyed. Many thousands of individual views can be called up on screen within seconds on one of the Frith internet sites, enabling people living continents away to revisit the streets of their ancestral home town, or view places in Britain where they have enjoyed holidays. Many overseas researchers welcome the chance to view special theme selections, such as transport, sports, costume and ancient monuments.

We are certain that Francis Frith would have heartily approved of these modern developments in imaging techniques, for he himself was always working at the very limits of Victorian photographic technology.

## The Value of the Archive Today

Because of the benefits brought by the computer, Frith's images are increasingly studied by social historians, by researchers into genealogy and ancestry, by architects, town planners, and by teachers and schoolchildren involved in local history projects.

In addition, the archive offers every one of us an opportunity to examine the places where we and our families have lived and worked down the years. Highly successful in Frith's own era, the archive is now, a century and more on, entering a new phase of popularity.

## The Past in Tune with the Future

Historians consider the Francis Frith Collection to be of prime national importance. It is the only archive of its kind remaining in private ownership and has been valued at a million pounds. However, this figure is now rapidly increasing as digital technology enables more and more people around the world to enjoy its benefits.

Francis Frith's archive is now housed in an historic timber barn in the beautiful village of Teffont in Wiltshire. Its founder would not recognize the archive office as it is today. In place of the many thousands of dusty boxes containing glass plate negatives and an all-pervading odour of photographic chemicals, there are now ranks of computer screens. He would be amazed to watch his images travelling round the world at unimaginable speeds through network and internet lines.

The archive's future is both bright and exciting. Francis Frith, with his unshakeable belief in making photographs available to the greatest number of people, would undoubtedly approve of what is being done today with his lifetime's work. His photographs, depicting our shared past, are now bringing pleasure and enlightenment to millions around the world a century and more after his death.

# The City of Norwich

Recently, the city fathers of Norwich chose a slogan that now adorns all the city entry road signs: 'A fine city'. It is indeed a fine city, despite Second World War bombing and wholesale 'improvement'. Like all modern cities, it is surrounded by suburbs in which can be found the remnants of older villages. It has a population of about 170,000. In the early 19th century, when almost all the city was still within the medieval walls, it had a population of about 35,000.

A Roman road once crossed the river Wensum at Caistor-by-Norwich where, it is thought, there was a government weaving works producing cloth for Roman army uniforms. Clearly, wool production has a very long history in East Anglia. The first real settlements in what is now Norwich were Anglo-Saxon. These grew sufficiently to ▶

**The City from St James's Hill 1896**  37342
This view looks across the city, past Cow Tower.
The great cathedral spire dominates the view, with
the square block of the castle on the left and St
Peter Mancroft's tower in between.

become a fortified burgh which by about 920 AD had its own mint, and had been given the name Norwic. It continued to grow; by 1066 it could sustain about 40 churches, and was the third largest port on the east coast of England after London and York.

After the Norman Conquest, more than 100 houses were cleared for the castle and more for a new market-place and the cathedral close area. The cathedral, or rather the bishop and the priory, arrived in 1094 when the see was transferred from Thetford. The city spread rapidly, and from the mid 13th until the mid 14th centuries, stone city walls were built with no less than 11 fortified gateways. The walls, stretches of which survive today, were about 2.5 miles long; they protected only three sides of the large medieval city - the fourth side was protected by a mile of the bank of the River Wensum. The medieval city grew up on the wool trade; it became one of England's wealthiest cities, with a population of about 15,000 by 1340. Indeed, until 1700 it was the second largest and wealthiest city after London.

The southern areas of the city, such as Ber Street and Rouen Road, were bombed and redeveloped with what can tactfully be termed mixed success; the huge number of surviving churches, as well as the cathedral and the intricate street pattern, give a quite remarkable feel of a medieval city. Escape from the continuous bustle is possible in the tranquil cathedral precincts. I hope that this collection of photographs gives a flavour of the city and encourages those who have never been to come, and those who know it already to take a fresh look.

▲ **The City**
**from above Pull's Ferry 1896** 37343
We are looking across the river Wensum, past the ancient Pull's Ferry named after a 19th-century ferryman; the cathedral and its precincts belie the industrial nature of late 19th-century Norwich.

◀ **Elm Hill 1929** 81804
Elm Hill was rescued from slum clearance by the Norwich Society in 1927 and beautifully restored. To those who see it now, the intended vandalism is difficult to comprehend.

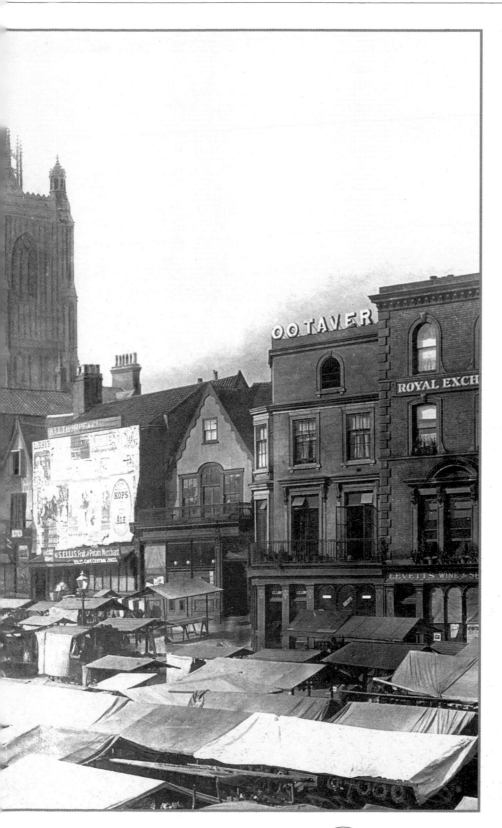

**The Market Place looking towards St Peter Mancroft's Church 1891** 29133 Between the Guildhall and St Peter Mancroft's church all the buildings on the right, except the Sir Garnet Wolseley pub, were demolished in the 1930s; the market was extended westwards to give the splendid new City Hall a prospect.

◀ **Elm Hill 1929** 81806
Now no longer a pub, the Britons Arms on the left, built as a community of religious women in the 15th century, was the only house to survive a great fire in 1507.

**◄ Elm Hill looking South-West 1929** 81805
In the 16th and 17th centuries, when these houses were built, the streets echoed to the hum of cloth looms. The buildings then became overcrowded housing for the woollen industry's factory workers, and after 1850, for shoe-factory workers.

**The Guildhall and the ►
War Memorial 1929**
81799
This jaunty flushwork of stone and flint diaper dates from the 1535 rebuild of the collapsed council chamber. The Lutyens war memorial was moved in 1938 to new memorial gardens in front of the new City Hall.

**The Guildhall and the ►
Market Place 1891** 28164
The seat of the medieval governance of the city, the Guildhall was built in 1407-13, but 1930s demolition in the market area has exposed the mainly Victorian south elevation to general view.

**The Market Place 1929** 81796
At this time, the buildings on the right are awaiting their fate - they were eventually pulled down. But they themselves had their origins in encroachment on the original larger medieval market place.

◄ **Rampant Horse Street looking South-East 1929** 81801
The columned and domed building in the distance on the right remains as part of Marks and Spencer. Everything else has gone; the buildings on the left were replaced by Debenhams in 1954.

◀ **Rampant Horse Street looking North-West 1891** 28163
This street was named after the Rampant Horse Inn, an old coaching inn. Not only have all the buildings in this view gone, but the street was also shortened to widen Red Lion Street.

▼ **Ber Street looking North 1891** 28162
Remarkably wide for Norwich, Ber Street was noted for its numerous butcheries and slaughterhouses. Only St John the Baptist's church and a couple of houses nearby escaped from the bombs intended for the port and the railway station.

◀ **Westlegate looking East 1890** 24044
All Saints Church in the distance is all that survived bombing and post-war clearance. At the time this photograph was taken, there was even a thatched pub, the quaintly-named Barking Dickey. It is difficult to equate this tumble-down cobbled street with today's unattractive Westlegate.

◄ **Royal Hotel and Post Office 1901** 46672
On the right are the old Post Office and the red brick and pedimented agricultural hall of 1882, both now occupied by Anglia Television. They are a fitting foil for the grandiose former Royal Hotel opposite, also partly occupied by Anglia Television.

◄ **The Post Office and Prince of Wales Road 1896** 37362
Prince of Wales Road was cut through the town in 1862 to provide a fittingly grand route from Thorpe Station. On the right, the old Crown Bank of 1866 became the post office.

**Davey Place 1922** ►
72602
Davey Place was formed in 1812 to link the cattle market (in Castle Meadow in front of the castle) with the main market place, butting through the yard of the King's Head. Unfortunately, the cast-iron framed building in the distance has long gone.

◄ **Bishopgate from across Bishops Bridge 1919** 69069
The medieval bridge, built about 1340, crosses the Wensum into Bishopgate, which ends with a gateway into the cathedral precinct. The Red Lion's conservatory has been replaced and stripped of the creeper.

◀ **Great Hospital, Bishopgate: St Helen's Square 1921** 70883 Originally intended for housing poor clergy, and other poor people, the hospital was founded by Bishop Walter de Suffield in 1249. Masses were to be said here for his soul in perpetuity.

◀ **Bishopgate looking West 1921**  70881
The cathedral precinct wall is on the left, and Great Hospital, founded in 1249 and with St Helen's Church attached to the Infirmary Hall, is opposite.

**Great Hospital: The** ▶
**Cloister 1921**  70885
The cloister lies to the north of the church, with the master's hall to its west. A small cloister, less than 60 ft square, it dates from about 1450; it is a tranquil, contemplative space.

◀ **Great Hospital and St Helen's Church 1921**
70882
The hospital was saved from dissolution under Henry VIII; Edward VI gave it to the city in 1547. The infirmary hall, rather quirkily, divides the long left-hand building with St Helen's Parish Church.

◄ **Strangers' Hall:
The Great Hall
and Minstrels Gallery
1901** 46683
This 15th-century hall
belonged to the
merchant William Barley.
It was modernised in
about 1530, and again in
1627, when the gallery
and stairs were inserted.

◀ **Strangers' Hall,
Charing Cross:
The Courtyard 1919**
69049
Strangers Hall was saved from demolition in 1899 by Leonard Bolingbroke, and was given to the city soon after this view was taken. It is one of the best medieval merchant houses in the city, and is now an excellent museum.

▼ **Strangers' Hall:
The Great Hall Bay
Window 1901**  46682
Outside the hall, Nicholas Sotherton's traceried bay window is flanked by Francis Cock's staircase bay of a century later. Both were added to a 15th-century structure.

◀ **Strangers' Hall:
The Panelled Room
1901**  46684
The panelled room is in one of the apartments that have been furnished as part of the museum. It shows urban life from the 16th to the 19th centuries.

**Nurse Cavell ▶
Memorial, Wensum
Street and Tombland
1929** 81819
The Edith Cavell
Memorial of 1918 was
originally erected in the
middle of Tombland. It
was moved in 1992 to a
plot beside the cathedral
precinct's Erpingham
Gate, presumably for its
own safety.

**▼ St Ethelbert's House,
Tombland 1929** 81808
This is a swagger Arts-
and-Crafts style house of
1888, with a welter of
mullions and transoms,
coving and gables. St
Ethelbert's House now
has a suitably ornate use
as Boswell's
brasserie/bar.

**▲ Maids Head Hotel,
Wensum Street 1901**
46681
Barely 12 years old at this
time, and still looking
pristine, this mock-Tudor
hotel was rebuilt and
reworked by Herbert
Green. The original hotel,
a jumble of buildings, was
certainly tidied up out of
all recognition.

**◄ Samson and Hercules House, Tombland 1929**

81810

In 1890, columns were replaced by these Jacobean figures to support the porch cornice. They are no longer there; the building is now a night club, with its own musclemen to guard the door.

# The Castle, the City Defences and the Parish Churches

Norwich's Norman castle keep is all that survives of the medieval castle buildings; it is a remarkable structure. Built around 1100 on a low hill, it replaced an earlier Norman timber castle. At over 70 ft high, it dominates many parts of the town; in fact, it dominates considerably more than the Cathedral, which is more prominent beyond the city. The castle seems to be an austere cube in distant views, but from closer to, the tier after tier of blind arches can be seen. All this work is new stone, put up when the castle was refaced in the 1830s. This is an accurate copy of the Norman work, but carried out in alien Bath stone, instead of the original pale Caen limestone from Normandy, which was brought by barges up the Wensum.

Attached to the castle is the old prison, built ▶

**Norwich Castle from the Old Cattle Market 1896** 37360
The old cattle market occupied part of the former bailey of the castle. In 1993 it was replaced by the very successful design of the Castle Mall shopping centre, partly built underground below a raised park.

in the 1820s on a radial plan; this was at the time the very latest in prison planning. The castle had actually been a gaol many centuries before, and certainly by the early 13th century. In 1887 the city bought the castle and converted the gaol into an art gallery and museum. The gallery has many fine works by the Norwich School of topographical artists, including John Sell Cotman and John Crome. In the first half of the 14th century, the city's timber defensive palisade, on an earthen bank behind a ditch, was wholly replaced in stone. Some idea of the scale of the enterprise can be given by raw statistics: there were 40 towers, 11 gateways, and more than 21.5 miles of 20 ft high wall. The wall had arcades supporting a wall-walk behind the battlements; it was fronted by ditches 20 ft deep and 60 ft across. Even so the walls did not surround the whole city, for the mile or so of the Wensum river frontage in the east has no walling. The best place to see surviving stretches of this great medieval enterprise is in Chapelfield Gardens. A number of towers survive. These include the pair of boom towers that raised a chain across the River Wensum to prevent enemy shipping penetrating the city, and, more splendidly, the isolated brick-faced Cow Tower of 1390, which defends a curve of the Wensum where there is no wall.

The other medieval glory of the city, apart from the cathedral of course, is its parish churches. An astonishing number survive, many with non-ecclesiastical uses now; but even so, few cities can rival this profusion. At its medieval peak, the city had 56 parish churches within the walls. There are still 31, although there were 36 before the Second World War. Five were destroyed by bombs. This dominance, combined with the old street patterns, give a remarkably medieval flavour to Norwich, despite an overwhelming majority of post-medieval secular buildings.

▲ **Norwich Castle Keep 1938** 88667
This view, showing the wonderful friezes of blind arcades, and with the 19th-century additions largely concealed, gives a good sense of the power of the keep on its mound.

◄ **Norwich Castle, The Lodges and The Bridge 1890**
24043
Francis Stone's 1811 lodges flank the main entrance to the castle. The bridge of 1825 replaced a crumbling 12th-century one. The austerity of this view is not softened by a few trees.

▼ **Norwich Castle, The Keep and The Gatehouse c1874** 7057
Nearer the castle the contrast between the Bath stone of the keep
and the crisp, pristine granite of the 1830s prison gatehouse is clear.
Taken 40 years after the prison was built, this is one of the earliest
views in the book.

▼ **Norwich Castle, The Bridge from Castle Gardens 1891** 29135
The deep medieval moat with its 1825 bridge was turned into delightful
gardens with terraces and benches. They remain virtually unchanged,
but away to the left is now the Castle Mall shopping centre.

▲ **The Boom Towers and
Carrow Bridge 1938**
88664
The boom towers
originally had a chain
stretched between them,
which could be raised to
block the River Wensum
if need be. Unfortunately,
the right-hand tower is
now only half the height it
was in this picture.

◀ **St Peter Mancroft's Church and Thomas Browne's Statue 1919**
69045
In 1905, Haymarket was turned into a grassed square, and standing in it was a statue of Sir Thomas Browne, the 17th-century religious thinker who lived nearby. It is sad that the grass has now gone.

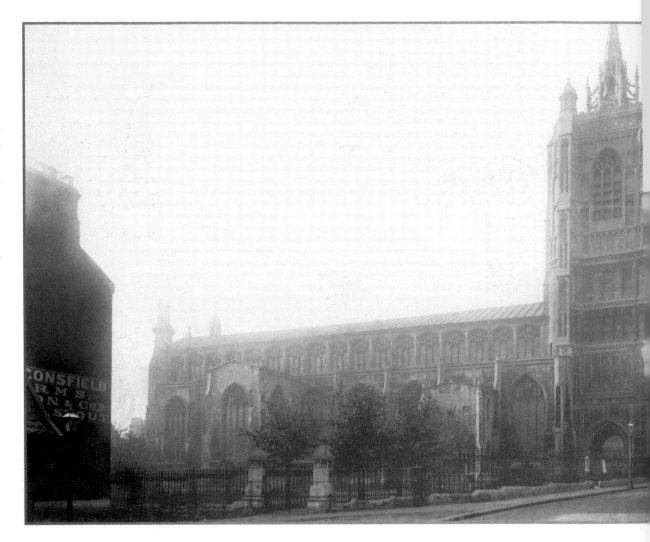

◀ **Cow Tower and the River Wensum 1891**

28158

The tower was rebuilt in flint faced with brick in about 1390, at the time when the city took it over from the Cathedral Priory. Originally in Cowholme Meadow, this unofficial dovecote is now within the well-treed riverside walk park.

**◄ St Peter Mancroft's Church 1896** 37365
This view, taken from Haymarket, shows the great parish church which dominates the west side of Norwich's great market-place. Haymarket is a smaller-scale market on the west side of the church.

**▼ St Giles's Church, St Giles Street 1891**
28170
This church, with its 120 ft high tower, occupies a large triangular churchyard. The 14th-century chancel was demolished in 1581, but rebuilt in 1867. The chief glory of the church is its early hammerbeam roof.

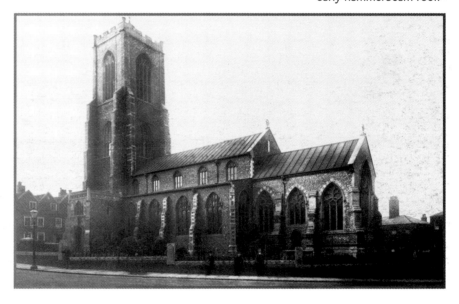

**◄ St Peter Parmentergate's Church, King Street 1891** 28171
In King Street, east of the castle, this church has been redundant since 1981. The church is an angular, aisleless flint building with a tall nave and an impressive west tower with stepped battlements.

▼ **St Michael-at-Thorn's, Ber Street 1891** 28169
St Michael's at Thorn was destroyed by bombs, so this is very much
an archive photograph. This view shows the church soon after
restoration work that added stepped battlements and removed a
south transept chapel.

▼ **St Michael-at-Plea's Church, Queen Street 1891** 28167
Made redundant, and disused for some years, this fine church is now a
craft centre. Mostly built in the usual flint with stone dressings, the two-
storey ashlar stone porch is particularly fine, and a little unusual for
Norwich.

▲ **St John the Baptist
Church, Interior 1896**
37363
At this stage only the
nave had been completed
in its austere early English
Gothic style. A temporary
wall separates it from the
crossing tower and the
dust from the building
works beyond the west
tower arch.

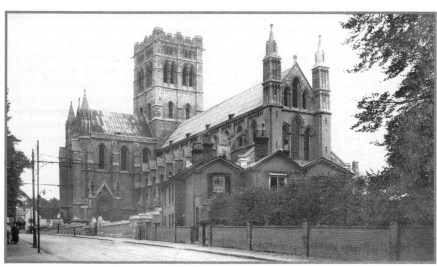

### ◀ St John the Baptist Church, Earlham Road 1919 69063

Now separated from the city by the inner ring road, this vast church was not built as a cathedral; it only became one in 1976. It was built for the Catholic 15th Duke of Norfolk between 1884 and 1910.

# Norwich Cathedral

The Cathedral Church of the Holy and Undivided Trinity, the Priory and The Precincts The city of Norwich has had its bishopric for 900 years; it was transferred from Thetford in 1094. The first bishop of Norwich, Herbert de Losinga, had bought the bishop of Thetford's mitre in 1091, along with the Abbacy of Winchester, from William Rufus, who was quite happy to sell ecclesiastical appointments. Thetford was too near the mighty Abbey of Bury St Edmunds, with whom the bishops of Thetford had been in near continuous dispute. Norwich had the undoubted advantage of being a long way from Bury, and had long been a thriving town. De Losinga arrived, and in the high-handed way of Norman aristocrats, promptly cleared a substantial part of the town to make his cathedral precinct. The foundation stone for Herbert's great cathedral was laid in 1096, and the east arm, the chancel, was ►

**The Cathedral from the Precinct Watergate and Pull's Ferry 1891** 28157
The medieval watergate was restored and roofed in 1947. The lane to Lower Close was originally a canal, used for carrying stone for building the cathedral.

ready for dedication in September 1101. De Losinga died in 1119 and never saw his great project completed; indeed, it had reached only the east part of the nave. It was completed by his successor in 1145.

Remarkably little has happened since, compared with the history of many other English cathedrals. The building is still essentially Norman, and only the great late 15th-century spire has materially changed distant views. It soars to 315 ft, the second highest spire in England after Salisbury. Its predecessor had been blown through the choir roof in a great gale in 1362; this also resulted in the building of the superb spacious clerestory of the choir.

The greatest and most successful and harmonious change to the Norman cathedral was the addition of stone vaults throughout, after a disastrous fire in 1463. The nave was done first, followed by the transepts and the choir, which were completed by 1500. It is astonishing that these intricate rib patterns and their glorious carved bosses complement the Norman work of 300 years before, but they undoubtedly do. The cathedral is one of the finest in England, and one of the most complete Norman ones. Herbert de Losinga and his successor, Eborard de Montgomery, would still feel at home.

Outside the cathedral there is a considerable acreage of green space within the precinct walls. The tranquil precincts are focused on Upper and Lower Closes. They run down to the River Wensum, and contain a considerable number of historic houses, as well as substantial remains of the pre-Reformation priory. Much of its medieval precinct wall survives, together with the watergate to the Wensum at Pull's Ferry and two medieval gatehouses into the town: truly a splendid legacy.

▼ **The Cathedral from the East c1874** 7054 This view, one of the earliest in the book, shows the east end of the cathedral with no east chapel, only ragged masonry. The Lady Chapel became ruinous in the 16th century and was pulled down.

▲ **The Cathedral from the South-East 1896**
37344
This view, looking across Lower Close, has changed remarkably little since 1896; it shows how the cathedral dominates its surroundings, towering over the houses of Lower Close.

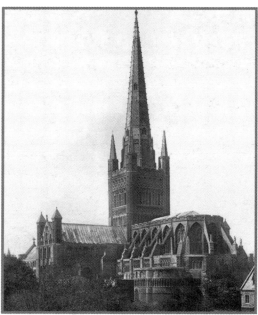

◄ **The Cathedral from the East 1896** 37347
The east arm of the cathedral has a lower Norman part, while the tall clerestory and flying buttresses are 14th-century; this is a direct consequence of an earlier spire falling through the chancel roof in 1362.

**The Cathedral:
The East End
and Nurse Cavell's
Grave 1919** 69040
Although the stonework
has been replaced since,
the heroic Edith Cavell's
grave is still a poignantly
simple one. She was
shot in Brussels by the
Germans in 1915 for
helping wounded British
soldiers escape the
country.

◀ **The Cathedral: The New Memorial Chapel and Edith Cavell's Grave 1932** 85102
On the right is the pristine stonework of the then new St Saviour's chapel; behind Nurse Cavell's cross is the two-storey Norman ambulatory chapel. In the foreground are the foundations of the 13th-century Lady Chapel.

▼ **The Cathedral from the North-East 1932**
85100
St Saviour's chapel at the east end was built between 1930 and 1932 as a First World War memorial. It replaced the long-demolished Lady Chapel, itself a 13th-century replacement for the Norman original.

◀ **The Cathedral from Lower Close 1891**
28140
This old view gives a fine impression of how long the cathedral is. The magnificent row of arched openings nearer the camera is the ruined priory infirmary.

**The Cathedral from the South 1922** 72597
Wonderful as this view is, admiration is tempered by the knowledge that the road leading to the south transept was created by the demolition in the 1830s of the mainly 12th-century monastic dormitory and chapter house.

**The Cathedral from the West 1896**
The west front is at the end of a very long fourteen-bay nave. The loss of its four tall turrets, seen in old prints, and vigorous 'improvements' and ill-considered 'corrections' have spoiled its original clean, well-balanced design.

**The Cathedral Interior: St Saviour's Chapel 1932**
The twin arches, with the quatrefoil over, are all that remain of the 13th-century Lady Chapel. In the foreground is the beautifully-cut stonework of St Saviour's Chapel, brand new at the time of this photograph.

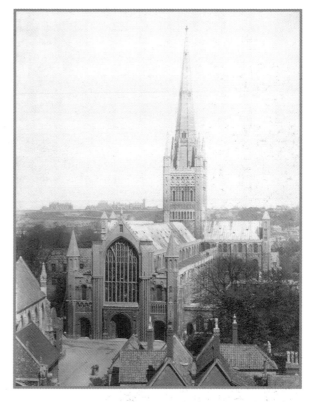

**The Cathedral from the West 1896** 37348

**The Cathedral Interior: St Saviour's Chapel 1932** 85105

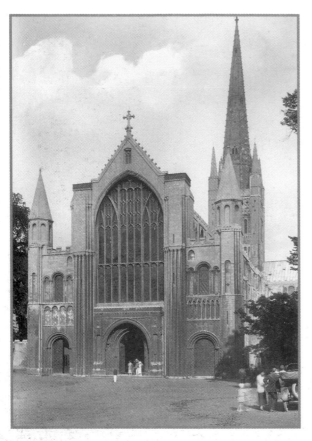

**The Cathedral, West Front 1922** 72596
Bishop Alnwick's 15th-century great west window is the most striking medieval alteration to the Norman west front. It floods the interior of the nave with light, filtered through stained glass.

**The Cathedral Interior: St Saviour's Chapel 1932** 85106
When it was newly-finished, the chapel was austere. Now it has elegant pews and an altar with fine medieval painted panels (from St Michael-at-Pleas Church), and is the regimental chapel of the Royal Norfolk Regiment containing their flags, honour and memorials.

**The Cathedral Interior: The Choir and the Crossing 1891** 28152
As is customary in medieval great churches, the choir stalls occupy the first bays of the nave. Norwich's date from 1420; but up to 1515 they had more than their fair share of fires, necessitating re-arrangements, renewals, repairs and additions.

◄ **The Cathedral Interior: The Choir looking West 1891** 28150
The great Norman crossing tower has windows high up, which flood the crossing with light. This view shows the Norman work well, with the network of 15th-century vault ribs receding into the distance.

◄ **The Cathedral Interior: The Choir looking West 1919**
69043
The organ over the pulpitum, the screen between choir stalls and nave, was installed in 1899 to replace the one of 1834 shown in photograph No 28152. Unfortunately, it too had to be rebuilt in 1938 after a fire.

◀ **The Precincts: The Cathedral from Lower Close 1938** 88670
The Deanery on the left and the terrace on the right of the north side of Lower Close both incorporate much medieval work. The terrace was converted from the priory granaries.

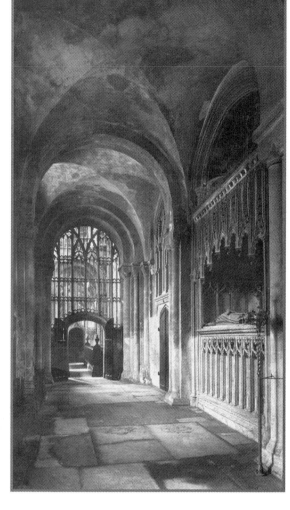

**The Cathedral ▶ Interior: South Choir Aisle 1891** 28153
The Norman choir and nave aisles were vaulted in stone from the start. The choir aisle vaults date from about 1100; they support the floor of the galleries above with their great arches.

◀ **The Precincts: The Cloister Court 1921** 70880
Norwich Cathedral's cloisters are, like its spire height, second in size only to Salisbury cathedral's. They were rebuilt slowly from 1297 to 1430; their size was set by the larger-than-life Herbert de Losinga's Norman cloisters, whose outer walls survived the 1272 fire.

◄ **The Precincts:
Upper Close and Lord
Nelson's Statue 1938**
88673
The precincts have two
closes. The western one
is architecturally less
interesting, but there are
statues of Wellington
and Nelson on the
green: Wellington's
moved here from the
market-place in 1937,
Nelson's in 1856.

◄ **The Precincts: The Cloister, East Walk 1891** 28154
The east walk of the cloisters were rebuilt first after the 1272 fire, and were completed by 1314. They end at the extraordinarily ornate doorway into the nave, the Prior's door, which dates from about 1310.

**The Cathedral ►
Interior: The Nave looking East 1891**
28147
Here we have a closer view of the pulpitum screen. Little of the original 15th-century stonework survived Anthony Salvin's 'restoration' in 1833. The nave vault has more than 250 bosses, all richly and superbly carved.

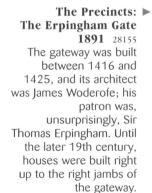

**The Precincts: ►
The Erpingham Gate 1891** 28155
The gateway was built between 1416 and 1425, and its architect was James Woderofe; his patron was, unsurprisingly, Sir Thomas Erpingham. Until the later 19th century, houses were built right up to the right jambs of the gateway.

◄ **The Cathedral Interior: The Nave Pulpit 1896** 37354
A fruity example of high Victorian exuberance, the nave pulpit dates from 1889. Behind it can be seen one of two spiral-cut columns. There were four, but the other two were altered after a fire in 1463.

◄ **The Precincts: Hook's Walk, off Lower Close 1922**

72598

At the east end, Lower Close leads into Hook's Walk with its excellent brick and flint-built houses, many rendered and colour-washed. It leads to the curiously-named Gooseberry Garden Walk.

**◄ The Precincts: Lower Close looking East 1938** 88674
The serene and tranquil Lower Close is surrounded by fine houses, mostly 'Georgianised', but incorporating priory buildings. This view is now obscured by the trees, which were newly-planted then, but have now matured.

**The Precincts: ►
The Ethelbert Gate
1891** 28156
This fine 14th-century gate rose from the ashes of the Norman one, burnt in the great riots of 1272. This view shows the 1815 restoration of the upper parts; the crumbling middle section was not restored until 1965.

**◄ The Cathedral Interior: The Nave looking East 1896** 37351
The immensely long nave has shafts and colonettes breaking its length, leading the eye up to the vaults. It is one of the masterpieces of medieval English architecture.

◄ **Cow Tower and the Wensum 1896** 37364
The Cow Tower, with barges moored nearby, looks out from the edge of Cowholme, now in the riverside walk park, to the late 19th-century city expansion beyond the Wensum.

# The River, the Parks and the City beyond the Walls

▲ **Bishops Bridge
over the River
Wensum 1891** 28159
In 1549, John Ket led his
rebel peasant army from
its camp on Mousehold
Heath over this fine
14th-century bridge,
only for his followers to
be cut to pieces in the
city. On the right is a
looming tannery, now
demolished.

In the past the River Wensum was the city's most
active trade route. South-east of the city it joined
the River Yare, which reaches the North Sea at
Yarmouth. The wealth of Norwich depended on
the river, for down it flowed its worsted and cloth
trade. Indeed, so great was the trade that during
the Middle Ages Norwich became the third most
important east-coast port; until about 1700,
Norwich was the second largest city in England.
The turnpike roads of the late 18th century, and
after 1844 the railway, reduced the importance of
the river to the newly-industrialised city, which by
now had textile, shoe-making, leather-working,
brewing and metal industries. But until the First
World War the river was humming with activity,
mostly sailing barges carrying bulky goods, raw
materials and local trade. Leisure boating took
over in the 1920s, and a yacht station was
established by Riverside Road. This is still ▶

immensely popular; for much of the year, Broads cruisers and boats tie up at the numerous moorings so that holiday-makers can visit the city. Historically, of course, the river was also a valued part of the city defences. The city grew in the river's loop, so that in effect the river was a wide wet moat along its east side. The defences included the boom towers south of Carrow Bridge, whose chain boom could be raised to close the river, preventing access upstream, and also the Cow Tower at the bend opposite St James' Hill. The cathedral precincts' watergate, known as Pull's Ferry after an Elizabethan ferryman, originally guarded the entrance to a canal that ran west into the Close: barges brought building stone from Normandy up the canal for the cathedral and priory.

Now the river bank has a splendid riverside walk from east of Whitefriars Bridge, through parks around Cow Tower and Pull's Ferry, to beyond the boom towers. The city has several municipal parks: these range from Chapelfield Gardens, laid out in 1877 by the city Corporation on an infilled reservoir, to the extraordinary Eaton Park of the 1920s in the suburbs. The most untamed public open space taken over by the city Corporation is the 180 acres of the famous Mousehold Heath, which was bought in the 1880s. The heath had originally been an area of about 6000 acres. Once Anglo-Saxon 'wildwood', most of it was enclosed in about 1800. The city's expansion, mostly this century, has absorbed a number of villages, including Heigham and Old Lakeham. In the process it has acquired an outer and an inner ring road, the University of East Anglia, and a population of more than 180,000. Despite all this, the city retains its qualities and its historic core: it is a city to be savoured, and visited and re-visited.

▲ **The Wensum and Riverside Road looking North from Prince of Wales Bridge 1901** 46678
By 1901, the Riverside Road development of the 1880s and 1890s was maturing. This view also shows the old towpath, with moored barges, prior to the improvements for pleasure boating.

**◄ The Wensum and the Yacht Station 1938** 88656
This view of Riverside Road was taken from Prince of Wales Bridge. By 1938, the trees planted in the 1880s were mature. The area beyond the Prince of Wales Bridge had been converted into the city yacht station for pleasure boats, although as can be seen from this photograph, barges remained at the warehouse opposite.

**The Diocesan Training College 1901** 46679
Originally founded for the training of school mistresses, the college continued until after the Second World War. By 1952, it had become a secondary modern school; it is now Parkside School.

▼ **The Wensum, looking towards Prince of Wales Bridge 1935** 86748
A sailing barge, once a common sight on the Broads and Norfolk rivers, is moored opposite the pleasure boats below the yacht station. One of these is a yacht, the other a river trip launch.

▼ **The Jenny Lind Hospital 1901** 46680
The old Jenny Lind Hospital, here shown soon after completion, commemorated the city's affection for Jenny Lind, the mid 19th-century soprano superstar known as The Swedish Nightingale, who was a popular and frequent visitor to Norwich.

▲ **Chapelfield Gardens 1901** 46688
Once belonging to the collegiate church of St Mary-in-the-Fields, this green was an unofficial park until 1877. Then the City Corporation filled in a reservoir and demolished the water tower to make this delightful park.

◀ **Chapelfield Gardens, The Pagoda and the Bandstand 1901** 46687
The 1880 bandstand now has a more interesting cupola roof. Beyond the bandstand is the Pagoda, a cast iron structure designed for the international Philadelphia Exhibition of 1876. It survived the war, but was removed in 1949.

◀ **Eaton Park,
The Lily Pond 1932**
85109
Eaton Park, out in the
western suburbs, has
three avenues and
rectangular ponds
converging on a
bandstand surrounded
by circular colonnaded
buildings, which were
built between 1924 and
1928. The columns and
balustrades are made of
pink cement, the rest
in grey.

◄ **Heigham, The Old Palace 1891** 28176
The Bishop's Palace was bomb-damaged in the Second World War; this view shows the 1615 front long before it had to be rebuilt. The building was once the Dolphin Inn; Bishop Hall lived here in the 1640s, hence the popular name.

▼ **Eaton Park, The Yacht Pond 1932** 85110
This view looks from the bandstand complex to the pavilion gateway. The park also has tennis courts, bowling greens, cricket pitches, flower gardens and a miniature railway: all the requirements for 1920s healthy outdoor leisure.

◄ **Earlham Hall 1938**
88655
Earlham Hall is a complex 16th- and 17th-century house in brick and flint, with early 18th-century shaped gables. It is now the School of Law of the University of East Anglia. It is screened from the modern university buildings by dense trees.

**Acle, The Green from the Post Office c1926** A204004
Acle is a small market town, now really a village; it was granted its market charter in the
13th century. It became a major cattle-market, receiving a boost when the railway arrived.

# Around Norwich
## Some Broads & River Villages

We have already seen the Wensum; moving east of Norwich, the rivers Yare and, to the north-east, the Bure and its tributaries, are the core of the Broads. These great areas of water, carrs and fens are now a major holiday centre, with hired boats, yachts, restored sailing barges, holiday-home boats, cruisers and all sorts of pleasure craft plying the lakes and waterways.

It is now known that the Broads are artificial. They are the water-filled holes left by a huge peat-digging industry. East Anglia in the Middle Ages was particularly short of timber for firewood, and the great city of Norwich in its midst had a voracious appetite for fuel for its industries, as well as for heating and cooking. Peat was the obvious answer, because there was plenty of it about; since the water table was lower until the late 13th century, peat digging alongside the rivers was straightforward.

A few statistics give an idea of the scale of the peat removal from the 10th to the 13th centuries: 900 million cubic feet of peat were removed at the rate of about 12 million turves a year. Norwich Cathedral Priory's kitchens alone consumed about 400,000 turves a year. After the spectacular surge of the North Sea in 1287, the industry declined. Successive sea surges drowned many of the peat pits, which gradually became unworkable. The Broads lakes are much smaller now than in 1300, because they have silted a lot to form carrs and reed fen - in short, these industrial diggings have become naturalised and beautiful. It is amazing that such a huge area of land could have been systematically removed, but the consequence is a distinctive and beautiful landscape, immensely popular for holidays. Indeed, it could be said that the popularity of the Broads threatens their survival, with pollution from field drainage and continuous wash from pleasure craft battering the banks.

The other famous features of the Broads area are the windmill pumps that lifted water from the flat drained landscape. Several have been beautifully restored, such as the Stracey Arms windpump near Acle. Drainage of the marshes got under way seriously after about 1750; the countryside became dotted with windmill water pumps, mostly along the river banks. At one time there were more than 200, but steam and then oil-driven pumps took over, although a few lingered in use until after the Second World War. Now electric pumps do the job.

▼ **Acle, The Street from the Green c1955** A204080
The Green is now tidied up, but it retains the signpost of Queen
Victoria's Golden Jubilee. This was the medieval market place of a
town strategically situated where the River Bure cut gently through
higher (for Norfolk) ground.

▼ **Acle, The Village from the Railway Bridge c1955** A204084
The A47 overpass bridge now replaces the buildings in the foreground,
but the church remains. Its characteristic East Anglian Norman round
tower is topped by an octagonal 13th-century belfry.

▲ **Acle, Fishing at Acle
Bridge c1929** A204037
Acle Bridge, a mile from
the village, crosses the
Bure. Two years after this
photograph was taken the
fine stone bridge, built in
about 1830, was replaced
by a steel one. This has
just been replaced
as well.

◀ **Acle, The Bridge Inn from Acle Bridge c1929**
A204024
Acle Bridge now has a thriving boatyard with leisure-boating facilities. The old Bridge Inn building has gone, but the pantiled outbuilding survives as a craft and gift shop.

◄ **Acle, The Bridge Inn, Acle Bridge c1955**

A204098

The now much enlarged thatched house on the right is the only Bridge Inn building standing today; the left-hand one has been demolished. Apparently, it incorporates some flinty remains of a small 13th-century priory.

### Acle, The Entrance to the River Thurne, near Thurne c1926
A204049
The River Thurne joins the Bure here, and both are excellent for sailing. The late 18th-century left-hand mill has lost its cap, but the 1820 Thurne Dyke mill on the right was beautifully restored in 1955.

### ▼ Acle, Clippesby Drain Windmill from Upton Dyke c1929 A204011
Now long-disused, this is one of many 19th-century pump mills built to lift water from the drained marshes. The mill has now lost its sails, but not its inverted boat-style cap.

### ◄ Brundall, The River Yare at Brundall Gardens 1922 72611
In the 1920s, these riverside gardens became extremely popular with Norwich citizens and trippers from further afield. Frederick Holmes Cooper created them, as well as arboreta and, of course, tea-rooms and a restaurant.

▼ **Brundall, Brundall Gardens 1922** 72613
Cooper had a steamship company for ferrying visitors to the gardens.
Here Cooper's house can be seen across the lily-covered lake. The
house has now gone, but the gardens, which fell into decay, are now
being restored.

▼ **Ludham, The Old Mill c1955** L110082
In this typical scene, a wherry sails past a disused early 19th-century
drainage windmill, typical of the 200 that once turned to keep the
marshes drained.

▲ **Ludham, Post Office
Corner c1955** L110075
Ludham is a crossroads
village set on higher
ground between the
rivers Thurne and Ant,
both tributaries of the
Bure. It is at the head of
its own tributary channel
to the Bure, Womack
Water.

◄ **Ludham, The Village, Catfield Road c1955**

L110076

The thatched house north of the crossroads no longer has a village shop. The outbuilding on the right is now The Cat's Whiskers, a hairdresser's whose name wittily puns on the road name.

▼ **Ludham, Main Street c1955** L110072
This range of 18th- and 19th-century cottages, some thatched, look
across to the parish church, whose churchyard wall can be seen on
the left. The village hardware shop is now the Alfresco Restaurant.

▼ **Thorpe St Andrew, Thorpe Reach on the River Yare 1899** 44478
A wherry breasts Thorpe Reach en route to Norwich past Thorpe St
Andrew. Here the Yare cuts close into a wooded 150 ft ridge, a view
now obscured by trees between village and river.

▲ **Thorpe St Andrew,
The Parish Church
from the Yare 1929**
81822
The parish church lost its
spire from bomb damage
in the Second World War.
This spire was itself a
Victorian replacement for
an old thatched one, now
a picturesque ruin in the
churchyard.

◄ **Thorpe St Andrew, St Andrew's Church Interior 1922** 72609
The new church was designed by Thomas Jekyll in 1866, and is a classic high Victorian angular, crisp monster. It has lots of different bright materials and extravagantly overscaled carved detail, such as the gigantic capitals dwarfing their columns.

◀ **Thorpe St Andrew, The Rush Cutters and the River Yare 1922**

72607

The Rush Cutters has a late 16th-century core, evident in the octagonal brick chimneys on the right and the massive stack behind the left hip. The houseboat is a real period piece.

**Thorpe St Andrew, The River Yare looking East 1919**

69075

This view looks downstream to the Rush Cutters pub from the south bank. The boating business is still there; it is now called Hearts Cruises, and has a wider range of boats than in 1919.

**Wroxham, The Broad 1934** 86359

Below Wroxham, the River Bure flows between several broads that form wonderful boating lakes. Being within a few miles of the village, they helped Wroxham become the major centre for cruising that it is today.

**Wroxham, on The Bure 1921** 70893

Wroxham is at the western gateway to the Broads, and profited greatly from the late 19th-century boom in 'messing about in boats'. J Loynes and Sons started the boom with their boatyard near the bridge.

▼ **Wroxham, At Wroxham Bridge c1955** W156145

Seen from the bridge, most of these buildings survive as cafes, gift shops, and the like. The prominent semi-circular gable on the right in the distance is the famous Roy's Stores.

▼ **Wroxham, The Crossroads c1955** W156113

Arnold Roy spotted the need for provisioning the Broads tourist industry early, and his story is a classic errand boy to shopping magnate story. This view shows the 1920s store with its deliberately eye-catching art deco gable.

▲ **Wroxham, Looking South c1955** W156112
Roy's main store is on the left, while the building beyond, also a Roy's shop, is now their bargain store. The building in the right foreground is now Roy's vast new supermarket.

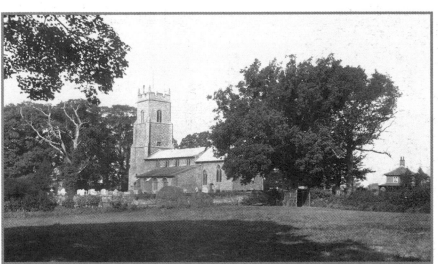

◀ **Wroxham, St Mary's Parish Church 1921**

70895

Well south of the bridge and 'Roytown', the parish church sits aloof. In the churchyard is the 1820s Mausoleum of the Traffords, the family of the long-demolished Wroxham Hall, whose gate lodge survives by the church.

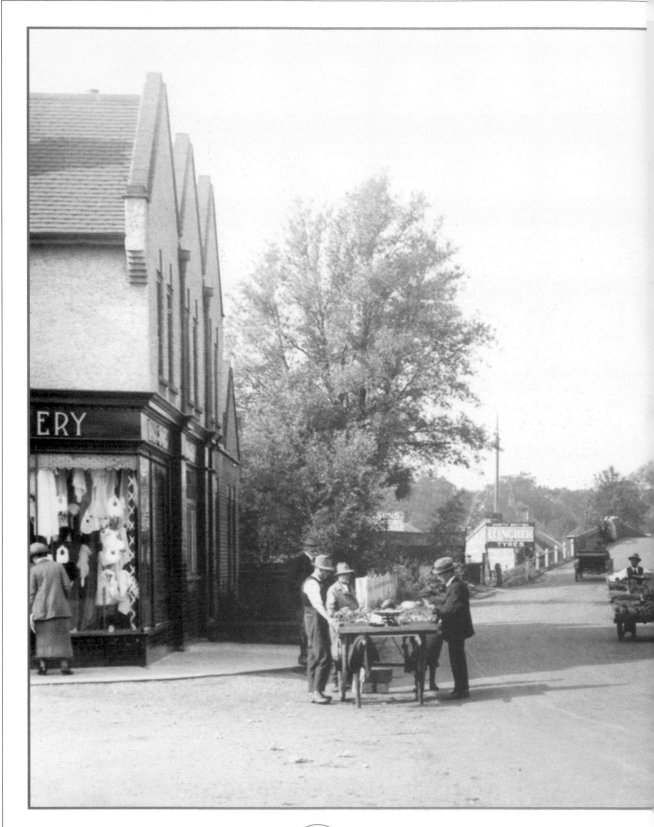

**Wroxham, Looking South to the Bridge over the Bure 1921**
70890
Both the buildings in the foreground are now part of the Roy empire; the battlemented one, oddly named 'Miss Roy', sells clothes. The original store is now a food hall and restaurant..

▼ **Aylsham, White Hart Street c1965** A220028
Aylsham prospered with linen manufacture in the Middle Ages, then
worsted weaving, before becoming an agricultural market town in the
18th century. The pub is now a house, but the street is relatively
unchanged.

▼ **Aylsham, The Market Place c1955** A220023
Thirteen miles from Norwich, Aylsham had a market by 1300, but
really developed later when John of Gaunt held the manor. His square
market place now has, on the left, a diminutive 19th-century town hall.

▲ **Aylsham, Red Lion
Lane c1955** A220002
Leading off the north-east
corner of the market-
place, Red Lion Lane
emphasises the local
market-town character of
Aylsham. It is still a town
serving an agricultural
community, and does not
depend upon tourism
alone.

◀ **Wymondham, The Market-Place and the Market Cross c1965**

W159035

Nine miles south-west of Norwich, Wymondham is noted for its fine priory church. The church was founded in 1107 and was the cause of bitter rivalry between town and prior, culminating in each faction building its own 15th-century bell towers.

◄ **North Walsham,
Market Street c1955**
N42024
The fine, large town
church is situated up an
alley at the east end of
Market Street and
behind the market-place.
Only remnants of its
medieval tower survive.
It collapsed in 1724, and
was never rebuilt.

### ◀ North Walsham, The Market Place 1921

70936

North Walsham is only 15 miles from Norwich; it prospered when Flemish weavers settled in the area in the 14th century. The fine timber-framed Market Cross of 1602 replaced the 1549 one, which was destroyed along with more than 100 houses in a disastrous fire in 1600.

### ▼ North Walsham, The Grammar School, c1955 N42015

South of the market-place, the old grammar school is centred around a wide, seven-bay red-brick building of 1765. It was founded before 1600; one of Norfolk's most celebrated sons, Horatio Nelson, was a pupil in the new building.

### ◀ North Walsham, Bactonwood Mill, Spa Common c1955 N42007

This was the former water mill. Smartened up, with its brickwork painted, the mill is now a house. It was powered by the head waters of the River Ant, canalised in 1826 as the North Walsham and Dilham Canal.

**Wymondham,
The Market Cross c1965**
The spacious market-place was
established by 1130, but the present
timber-framed 'cross' building dates from
1617. It replaced the original after yet
another Norfolk fire gutted the
town centre.

**Wymondham, The Green Dragon,
Church Street c1965**
On the road leading to the priory
gateway, this fine 14th-century, jettied,
timber-frame building may have been
built for visitors to the abbey. The period
petrol pumps have now gone.

**Wymondham, The Market Cross c1965** W159040

**Wymondham, The Green Dragon, Church Street c1965** W159027

# Index

# Frith Book Co Titles

Frith Book Company publish over 100 new titles each year. For latest catalogue please contact Frith Book Co.

Town Books 96pp, 100 photos. County and Themed Books 128pp, 150 photos
(unless specified) All titles hardback laminated case and jacket
except those indicated pb (paperback)

| | | | | | | |
|---|---|---|---|---|---|---|
| Around Bakewell | 1-85937-113-2 | £12.99 | | Isle of Man | 1-85937-065-9 | £14.99 |
| Around Barnstaple | 1-85937-084-5 | £12.99 | | Isle of Wight | 1-85937-114-0 | £14.99 |
| Around Bath | 1-85937-097-7 | £12.99 | | Around Leicester | 1-85937-073-x | £12.99 |
| Around Blackpool | 1-85937-049-7 | £12.99 | | Around Lincoln | 1-85937-111-6 | £12.99 |
| Around Bognor Regis | 1-85937-055-1 | £12.99 | | Around Liverpool | 1-85937-051-9 | £12.99 |
| Around Bournemouth | 1-85937-067-5 | £12.99 | | Around Maidstone | 1-85937-056-X | £12.99 |
| Around Bristol | 1-85937-050-0 | £12.99 | | North Yorkshire | 1-85937-048-9 | £14.99 |
| British Life A Century Ago | | | | Northumberland and Tyne & Wear | | |
| | 1-85937-103-5 | £17.99 | | | 1-85937-072-1 | £14.99 |
| Around Cambridge | 1-85937-092-6 | £12.99 | | Around Nottingham | 1-85937-060-8 | £12.99 |
| Cambridgeshire | 1-85937-086-1 | £14.99 | | Around Oxford | 1-85937-096-9 | £12.99 |
| Cheshire | 1-85937-045-4 | £14.99 | | Oxfordshire | 1-85937-076-4 | £14.99 |
| Around Chester | 1-85937-090-X | £12.99 | | Around Penzance | 1-85937-069-1 | £12.99 |
| Around Chesterfield | 1-85937-071-3 | £12.99 | | Around Plymouth | 1-85937-119-1 | £12.99 |
| Around Chichester | 1-85937-089-6 | £12.99 | | Around Reading | 1-85937-087-X | £12.99 |
| Cornwall | 1-85937-054-3 | £14.99 | | Around St Ives | 1-85937-068-3 | £12.99 |
| Cotswolds | 1-85937-099-3 | £14.99 | | Around Salisbury | 1-85937-091-8 | £12.99 |
| Cumbria | 1-85937-101-9 | £14.99 | | Around Scarborough | 1-85937-104-3 | £12.99 |
| Around Derby | 1-85937-046-2 | £12.99 | | Scottish Castles | 1-85937-077-2 | £14.99 |
| Devon | 1-85937-052-7 | £14.99 | | Around Sevenoaks and Tonbridge | | |
| Dorset | 1-85937-075-6 | £14.99 | | | 1-85937-057-8 | £12.99 |
| Dorset Coast | 1-85937-062-4 | £14.99 | | Sheffield and S Yorkshire | | |
| Down the Thames | 1-85937-121-3 | £14.99 | | | 1-85937-070-5 | £14.99 |
| Around Dublin | 1-85937-058-6 | £12.99 | | Around Southport | 1-85937-106-x | £12.99 |
| East Anglia | 1-85937-059-4 | £14.99 | | Around Shrewsbury | 1-85937-110-8 | £12.99 |
| Around Eastbourne | 1-85937-061-6 | £12.99 | | Shropshire | 1-85937-083-7 | £14.99 |
| English Castles | 1-85937-078-0 | £14.99 | | South Devon Coast | 1-85937-107-8 | £14.99 |
| Essex | 1-85937-082-9 | £14.99 | | Staffordshire | 1-85937-047-0 (96pp) | £12.99 |
| Around Exeter | 1-85937-126-4 | £12.99 | | Around Stratford upon Avon | | |
| Around Falmouth | 1-85937-066-7 | £12.99 | | | 1-85937-098-5 | £12.99 |
| Around Great Yarmouth | | | | Suffolk | 1-85937-074-8 | £14.99 |
| | 1-85937-085-3 | £12.99 | | Surrey | 1-85937-081-0 | £14.99 |
| Greater Manchester | 1-85937-108-6 | £14.99 | | Around Torbay | 1-85937-063-2 | £12.99 |
| Hampshire | 1-85937-064-0 | £14.99 | | Welsh Castles | 1-85937-120-5 | £14.99 |
| Around Harrogate | 1-85937-112-4 | £12.99 | | West Midlands | 1-85937-109-4 | £14.99 |
| Hertfordshire | 1-85937-079-9 | £14.99 | | Wiltshire | 1-85937-053-5 | £14.99 |

# Frith Book Co Titles Available in 2000

| | | | |
|---|---|---|---|
| Canals and Waterways | 1-85937-129-9 | £17.99 | Apr |
| Around Guildford | 1-85937-117-5 | £12.99 | Apr |
| Around Horsham | 1-85937-127-2 | £12.99 | Apr |
| Around Ipswich | 1-85937-133-7 | £12.99 | Apr |
| Ireland (pb) | 1-85937-181-7 | £9.99 | Apr |
| London (pb) | 1-85937-183-3 | £9.99 | Apr |
| New Forest | 1-85937-128-0 | £14.99 | Apr |
| Around Newark | 1-85937-105-1 | £12.99 | Apr |
| Around Newquay | 1-85937-140-x | £12.99 | Apr |
| Scotland (pb) | 1-85937-182-5 | £9.99 | Apr |
| Around Southampton | 1-85937-088-8 | £12.99 | Apr |
| Sussex (pb) | 1-85937-184-1 | £9.99 | Apr |
| Around Winchester | 1-85937-139-6 | £12.99 | Apr |
| | | | |
| Around Belfast | 1-85937-094-2 | £12.99 | May |
| Colchester (pb) | 1-85937-188-4 | £8.99 | May |
| Dartmoor | 1-85937-145-0 | £14.99 | May |
| Exmoor | 1-85937-132-9 | £14.99 | May |
| Leicestershire (pb) | 1-85937-185-x | £9.99 | May |
| Lincolnshire | 1-85937-135-3 | £14.99 | May |
| North Devon Coast | 1-85937-146-9 | £14.99 | May |
| Nottinghamshire (pb) | 1-85937-187-6 | £9.99 | May |
| Peak District | 1-85937-100-0 | £14.99 | May |
| Redhill to Reigate | 1-85937-137-x | £12.99 | May |
| Around Truro | 1-85937-147-7 | £12.99 | May |
| Yorkshire (pb) | 1-85937-186-8 | £9.99 | May |
| | | | |
| Berkshire (pb) | 1-85937-191-4 | £9.99 | Jun |
| Brighton (pb) | 1-85937-192-2 | £8.99 | Jun |
| Churches of Berkshire | 1-85937-170-1 | £17.99 | Jun |
| Churches of Dorset | 1-85937-172-8 | £17.99 | Jun |
| Derbyshire (pb) | 1-85937-196-5 | £9.99 | Jun |
| East Sussex | 1-85937-130-2 | £14.99 | Jun |
| Edinburgh (pb) | 1-85937-193-0 | £8.99 | Jun |
| Norwich (pb) | 1-85937-194-9 | £8.99 | Jun |
| South Devon Living Memories | | | |
| | 1-85937-168-x | £14.99 | Jun |

| | | | |
|---|---|---|---|
| Stone Circles & Ancient Monuments | | | |
| | 1-85937-143-4 | £17.99 | Jun |
| Victorian & Edwardian Kent | | | |
| | 1-85937-149-3 | £14.99 | Jun |
| Warwickshire (pb) | 1-85937-203-1 | £9.99 | Jun |
| | | | |
| Buckinghamshire (pb) | 1-85937-200-7 | £9.99 | Jul |
| Kent (pb) | 1-85937-189-2 | £9.99 | Jul |
| Kent Living Memories | 1-85937-125-6 | £14.99 | Jul |
| Victorian & Edwardian Yorkshire | | | |
| | 1-85937-154-x | £14.99 | Jul |
| West Sussex | 1-85937-148-5 | £14.99 | Jul |
| | | | |
| Cornish Coast | 1-85937-163-9 | £14.99 | Aug |
| County Durham | 1-85937-123-x | £14.99 | Aug |
| Croydon Living Memories | | | |
| | 1-85937-162-0 | £12.99 | Aug |
| Dorsert Living Memories | | | |
| | 1-85937-210-4 | £14.99 | Aug |
| Down the Severn | 1-85937-118-3 | £14.99 | Aug |
| Folkstone | 1-85937-124-8 | £12.99 | Aug |
| Glasgow (pb) | 1-85937-190-6 | £8.99 | Aug |
| Gloucestershire | 1-85937-102-7 | £14.99 | Aug |
| Herefordshire | 1-85937-174-4 | £14.99 | Aug |
| Lancashire (pb) | 1-85937-197-3 | £9.99 | Aug |
| Manchester (pb) | 1-85937-198-1 | £8.99 | Aug |
| Margate, Ramsgate & Broadstairs | | | |
| | 1-85937-116-7 | £12.99 | Aug |
| North London | 1-85937-206-6 | £14.99 | Aug |
| Picturesque Harbours | 1-85937-208-2 | £17.99 | Aug |
| Somerset | 1-85937-153-1 | £14.99 | Aug |
| Teeside | 1-85937-211-2 | £14.99 | Aug |
| Worcestershire | 1-85937-152-3 | £14.99 | Aug |
| Victorian & Edwardian Maritime Album | | | |
| | 1-85937-144-2 | £17.99 | Aug |
| Yorkshire Living Memories | | | |
| | 1-85937-166-3 | £14.99 | Aug |

# Available from your local bookshop or from the publisher

# FRITH PRODUCTS & SERVICES

Francis Frith would doubtless be pleased to know that the pioneering publishing venture he started in 1860 still continues today. More than a hundred and thirty years later, The Francis Frith Collection continues in the same innovative tradition and is now one of the foremost publishers of vintage photographs in the world. Some of the current activities include:

## Interior Decoration

Today Frith's photographs can be seen framed and as giant wall murals in thousands of pubs, restaurants, hotels, banks, retail stores and other public buildings throughout the country. In every case they enhance the unique local atmosphere of the places they depict and provide reminders of gentler days in an increasingly busy and frenetic world.

## Product Promotions

Frith products have been used by many major companies to promote the sales of their own products or to reinforce their own history and heritage. Brands include Hovis bread, Courage beers, Scots Porage Oats, Colman's mustard, Cadbury's foods, Mellow Birds coffee, Dunhill pipe tobacco, Guinness, and Bulmer's Cider.

## Genealogy and Family History

As the interest in family history and roots grows world-wide, more and more people are turning to Frith's photographs of Great Britain for images of the towns, villages and streets where their ancestors lived; and, of course, photographs of the churches and chapels where their ancestors were christened, married and buried are an essential part of every genealogy tree and family album.

A series of easy-to-use CD Roms is planned for publication, and an increasing number of Frith photographs will be able to be viewed on specialist genealogy sites. A growing range of Frith books will be available on CD.

## Frith Products

All Frith photographs are available Framed or just as Mounted Prints, and can be ordered from the address below. From time to time other products - Address Books, Calendars, Table Mats, etc - are available.

## The Internet

Already thousands of Frith photographs can be viewed and purchased on the internet. By the end of the year 2000 some 60,000 Frith photographs will be available on the internet. The number of sites is constantly expanding, each focussing on different products and services from the Collection.

Some of the sites are listed below.

www.townpages.co.uk
www.icollector.com
www.barclaysquare.co.uk
www.cornwall-online.co.uk

For more detailed information on Frith companies and products, look at these sites:

www.francisfrith.co.uk
www.frithbook.co.uk
www.francisfrith.com

---

### See the complete list of Frith Books at:

#### www.frithbook.co.uk

This web site is regularly updated with the latest list of publications from the Frith Book Company Ltd. If you wish to buy books relating to another part of the country that your local bookshop does not stock, you may purchase on-line.

---

*For further information, trade, or author enquiries please contact us at the address below:*
**The Francis Frith Collection, Frith's Barn, Teffont, Salisbury, Wiltshire, England SP3 5QP.**
Tel: +44 (0)1722 716 376  Fax: +44 (0)1722 716 881  Email: uksales@francisfrith.com

# To receive your FREE Mounted Print

**Mounted Print**
*Overall size 14 x 11 inches*

*Cut out this Voucher and return it with your remittance for £1.50 to cover postage and handling.*

*Choose any photograph included in this book. Your SEPIA print will be A4 in size, and mounted in a cream mount with burgundy rule lines, overall size 14 x 11 inches.*

## Order additional Mounted Prints at HALF PRICE (only £7.49 each*)

If there are further pictures you would like to order, possibly as gifts for friends and family, acquire them at half price (no additional postage and handling required).

## Have your Mounted Prints framed*

For an additional £14.95 per print you can have your chosen Mounted Print framed in an elegant polished wood and gilt moulding, overall size 16 x 13 inches (no additional postage and handling required).

---

**\* IMPORTANT!**
**These special prices are only available if ordered using the original voucher on this page (no copies permitted) and at the same time as your free Mounted Print, for delivery to the same address**

---

## Frith Collectors' Guild

*From time to time we publish a magazine of news and stories about Frith photographs and further special offers of Frith products. If you would like 12 months FREE membership, please return this form.*

*Send completed forms to:*
**The Francis Frith Collection, Frith's Barn, Teffont, Salisbury, Wiltshire SP3 5QP**

---

# *Voucher* for FREE and Reduced Price Frith Prints

| Picture no. | Page number | Qty | Mounted @ £7.49 | Framed + £14.95 | Total Cost |
|---|---|---|---|---|---|
| | | 1 | **Free of charge*** | £ | £ |
| | | | £7.49 | £ | £ |
| | | | £7.49 | £ | £ |
| | | | £7.49 | £ | £ |
| | | | £7.49 | £ | £ |
| | | | £7.49 | £ | £ |

| *Please allow 28 days for delivery* | * Post & handling | £1.50 |
|---|---|---|
| **Book Title** . . . . . . . . . . . . . . . | **Total Order Cost** | £ |

***Please do not photocopy this voucher. Only the original is valid, so please cut it out and return it to us.***

I enclose a cheque / postal order for £ . . . . . . . . . . made payable to 'The Francis Frith Collection'
OR please debit my Mastercard / Visa / Switch / Amex card

Number . . . . . . . . . . . . . . . . . . . . . . . . . . . . .

Expires . . . . . . . . . .   Signature . . . . . . . . . . . . . .

Name  Mr/Mrs/Ms . . . . . . . . . . . . . . . . . . . . . . . . . . .

Address . . . . . . . . . . . . . . . . . . . . . . . . . . . . . . . . . .

. . . . . . . . . . . . . . . . . . . . . . . . . . . . . . . . . . . . . . . . .

. . . . . . . . . . . . . . . . . . . . . . . . . . . . . . . . . . . . . . . . .

. . . . . . . . . . . . . . . . . . Postcode . . . . . . . . . . . . . . .

Daytime Tel No . . . . . . . . . . . . . . . . . . . . . .     Valid to 31/12/01

---

# The Francis Frith Collectors' Guild

Please enrol me as a member for 12 months free of charge.

Name  Mr/Mrs/Ms . . . . . . . . . . . . . . . . . . . . . . . . . . .

Address . . . . . . . . . . . . . . . . . . . . . . . . . . . . . . . . . .

. . . . . . . . . . . . . . . . . . . . . . . . . . . . . . . . . . . . . . . . .

. . . . . . . . . . . . . . . . . Postcode . . . . . . . . . . . . . . .

Free Print - see overleaf